An exciting new game-like way to learn how chords
made and played on all popular chord instruments

The name of the game is

Chord

BINGO

by Dick Sheridan

A do-it-yourself method that shows how to make
virtually every type of chord used today
in traditional and modern harmony.

Explains scales, inversions, generic chords, jazz chords, and
gives dozens of chord possibilities in every key. Provides detailed guidelines
along with useful terms, helpful charts
and diagrams.

EASY***EDUCATIONAL***FUN

ISBN 978-1-57424-359-8
SAN 683-8022

Cover by James Creative Group

Copyright © 2017 CENTERSTREAM Publishing, LLC
P.O. Box 17878 - Anaheim Hills, CA 92817

www.centerstream-usa.com | centerstrm@aol.com

ACKNOWLEDGMENTS

Many people have contributed in one form or another to the development of this book, and to all I am very grateful. Special thanks is due to the drafters of fretboard diagrams, namely Joe Steinman and Larry Czajkowski, while Wendi Ackerman created spreadsheet tables, charts, and inserts far beyond the author's graphic abilities. Together we made it happen.

And there are others -- students, friends, and music colleagues alike -- who over the years have offered support and invaluable help. Thanks too to Josepth McNaughton from B. M. G. magazine for that delightful London afternoon in 1970. His initial encouragement and sustained enthusiasm for Chord Bingo is remembered and appreciated.

To these and more, please know my gratitude.

Dick Sheridan

~CONTENTS~

INTRODUCTION

It is always surprising to find that many players of chord instruments have very little idea of just what it is they are playing. They have learned to form certain chords mechanically and to use them only as indicated by accompanying chord symbols or diagrams. The meaning of a chord name or what tones it represents is often a mystery to them.

Many of these instrumentalists play quite passably, and perhaps the question might be raised: if one can play chords well without knowledge of chord theory, why go further? The answer is unqualified: a better understanding can help you become a more versatile, accomplished musician.

Suppose, for example, you come across a chord name or symbol that calls for an unfamiliar chord but does not provide a diagram (also called a frame) or spell out its chord tones. Or perhaps there are better sounding inversions for chords you already know. Maybe you'd like to know how to form certain chords on instruments other than your own when no chord collections or guides are available. CHORD BINGO to the rescue! Using easy theory you'll be able to construct the chord yourself. It's basically simple: you select a scale and then extract certain tones from it.

Only a few steps are required:
1. Pick a chord
2. Determine the required scale and tone numbers
3. Using a scale chart, convert those numbers to letters
4. Arrange those letters on a fretboard or keyboard diagram.
   BINGO! You now have a chord!

Each of these steps will be thoroughly explained together with tips and terms to aid your complete understanding and to increase your feel for the subject. No matter what type of instrument you now play, no matter what kind of music you prefer, this novel approach to learning can do much to increase your knowledge of music in general and chords in particular.

Okay, now let's get started. Here's the first thing to understand, it's the BASIC RULE:

CHORDS ARE MADE FROM SCALES

But what is a scale? Simply put, it's a series of tones arranged in either ascending or descending order, like going up and down a ladder. It's the do-re-mi-fa-sol-la-ti-do that you learned in grade school music class. Eight notes that start on a pitch and climb up or down to the note of the same name. That interval is called an OCTAVE. Makes sense. "Octo" means eight, like an octopus with eight arms or an octagon with eight sides. Even the month of October used to be the eighth month until the Romans rearranged the calendar and honored Julius Caesar and Octavian Augustus by inserting July and August.

Here's an example of a scale starting with C on the keyboard and playing only the white notes: C-D-E-F-G-A-B-C. Now let's put a number on each of these notes: C=1, D=2, E=3, F=4, G=5, A=6, B=7, the octave C=8, which is essentially the same as 1.

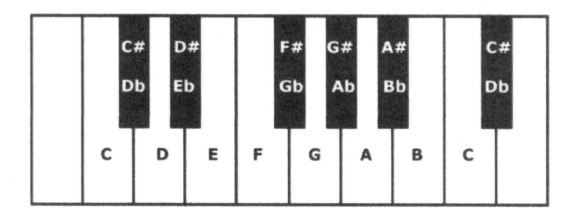

By combining certain tones we'll have a chord. A chord, incidentally, is three or more tones played together. If you combine the 1st, 3rd, and 5th scale tones you have a chord called a "major" chord. Referring to the scale we've just seen those tones would be C-E-G. You've now made your first chord, a C major chord. Easy, huh?

Notice on the keyboard diagram that the black notes have two names, a sharp (#) and a flat (b). These tones are called ENHARMONIC, meaning they have the same pitch but different names. A black note higher than a corresponding white note uses the sharp, while a black note lower than a corresponding white note uses a flat. There is no black note between B and C or between E and F. Consequently there is usually no B# or Cb, no E# or Fb. This applies not only to the keyboard but to all other instruments as well.

Back to the C chord we just made. It has only three tones, you say. What do we do with a 4-string instrument or one with five strings, or even six strings like a guitar? Or a keyboard? The answer is that some tones have to be doubled or tripled an octave or two apart. You might have two Cs, or a couple of Gs, or maybe three Es. On a string instrument, of course, those duplicated tones would be played on different strings.

GUITAR

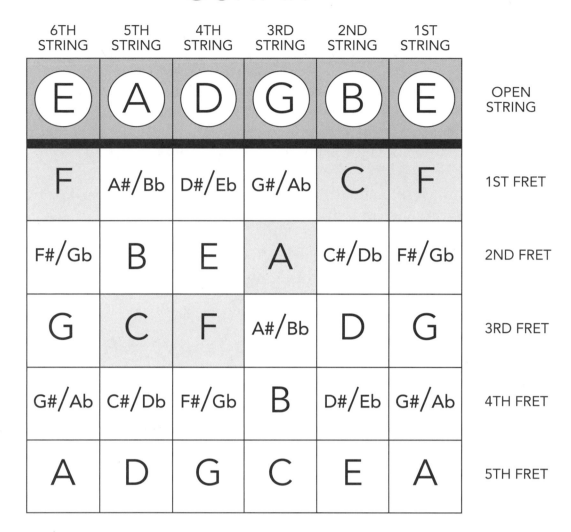

	6TH STRING	5TH STRING	4TH STRING	3RD STRING	2ND STRING	1ST STRING	
	E	A	D	G	B	E	OPEN STRING
	F	A#/Bb	D#/Eb	G#/Ab	C	F	1ST FRET
	F#/Gb	B	E	A	C#/Db	F#/Gb	2ND FRET
	G	C	F	A#/Bb	D	G	3RD FRET
	G#/Ab	C#/Db	F#/Gb	B	D#/Eb	G#/Ab	4TH FRET
	A	D	G	C	E	A	5TH FRET

The diagram above shows an F major chord and how it can be played on the guitar. We'll find later that this chord calls for three different tones:

F-C-A. See how the F note is tripled – they'd be octaves apart -- on the 6th, 4th, and 1st string. Did you notice that the C note is doubled on the 5th and 2nd string? (Strings shown on the diagram are numbered from left to right: 6=low E, 5=A, 4=D, 3=G, 2=B, and 1=-high E.)

With a more complex chord of 4 or more tones, sometimes a tone has to be eliminate to fit into an instrument that has fewer strings than chord tones. But more too of that later.

You probably already know that the musical alphabet starts on A and continues in alphabetical order: A-B-C-D-E-F-G and then starts all over again with A. There is no H-I-J-K and so on (except in Germany where H=B.)

Scales can start on any one of those alphabet tones, but sometimes we have to alter a tone in the scale making it higher or lower by using a sharp (#) to raise a pitch or a flat (b) to lower it. Scales too can be based on these altered tones, most commonly using flats in their name like the scale of Ab, or Bb, or Eb.

There are two different types of scales with which we are concerned in chord construction. One is called a CHROMATIC scale, the other a DIATONIC scale.

THE CHROMATIC SCALE

A chromatic scale consists of 12 tones which are arranged in half steps (also called half tones or semitones). They are the smallest interval in our Western system of music. Starting with any note in the musical alphabet, the chromatic scale proceeds in consecutive half-steps – baby steps, if you will -- until the note of the same name above or below the starting note is reached.

Half tones are like going from a white note to a black note on a piano keyboard or from consecutive frets on a string of a fretted string instrument.

Let's illustrate the chromatic scale of C. We'll start with C and use every possible tone between it and the C above. Climbing up the scale like this, going to higher and higher pitches, is called ascending. Here are the steps:

C-C#-D-D#-E-F-F#-G-G#-A-A#-B-C

Observe that there are 12 steps in the chromatic scale before the upper C is reached. Notice too that the steps proceed in alphabetical order. The "sharp" notes (the ones with a #) take their name from the letter that precedes them.

A descending scale reverses the note order and uses flats. Flats, we've seen, are indicated with a small "b" and take their name from the note that precedes them. Reading from left to right, here's the descending chromatic scale of C:

C-B-Bb-A-Ab-G-Gb-F-E-Eb-D-Db-C

Again, there are 12 steps before the lower C octave is reached. Don't forget that on the keyboard there is no black note between E and F and also between B and C. Consequently there is no Fb or Cb.

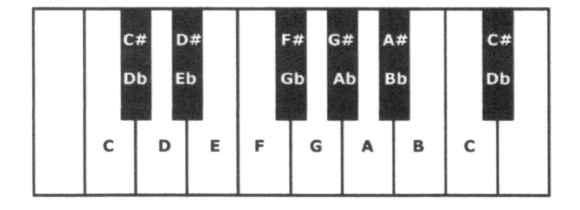

If we use the highest pitched guitar string (called the 1st string) to further illustrate half-tones, the open string is an E, the 1st fret an F, the 2nd fret an F# (or Gb), the 3rd fret a G, the 4th fret a G# (or Ab), the 5th fret an A, the 6th fret an A# (or Bb), the 7th fret a B, the 8th fret a C, and so on, climbing fret by fret until the next E is reached on the 12th fret.

Frets are actually the thin metal dividers of the fingerboard.   But for our use the term refers to the space between the metal dividers. Thus the first space is called the first fret, the second space the second fret, and so on.

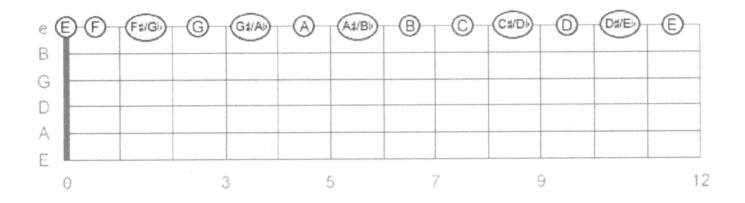

For the most frequently used chromatic scales, see the chart CHROMATIC SCALES WITH DIATONIC SCALES HIGHLIGHTED that is provided in this book.

The Nat King Cole Trio

9

THE DIATONIC SCALE

This scale consists of eight tones, those do-re-mi-fa-sol-la ti-do's that we've already mentioned. Its eight tones start on a note and climb up or go down to the note of the same name.

Unlike the 12-tone chromatic scale whose intervals are entirely in half steps, the 8-tone diatonic scale consists of two whole steps, a half step, then three whole steps and another half step. A whole step is made up of two half steps. In numbers the sequence looks like this:

$$2\text{-}\tfrac{1}{2}\text{-}3\tfrac{1}{2}$$

This formula can be applied to any chromatic scale to determine its diatonic equivalent. Therefore the diatonic scale of C is:

C-D-E-F-G-A-B-C.

C to D is a whole step
D to E is a whole step
E to F is a half-step
F to G is a whole step
G to A is a whole step
A to B is a whole step
B to C is a half-step

Look back to the piano keyboard diagram and you'll see that the scale consists of just the white notes from C to C. Any other scale will have at least one black note.

For chord construction we use the diatonic scale which is extracted from the chromatic scale.

NOTE: When using the chromatic scale to form the diatonic scale make sure that scale tones are consecutively alphabetical. Here's the chromatic scale of F which we'll use to make the diatonic scale of F.

F-F#-G-G#-A-A#-B-C-C#-D-D#-E-F.

Using our 2-½-3-½ formula we come out with: F-G-A-A#-C-D-E-F. But to keep the alphabet consecutive we need to change the A# to Bb, its enharmonic equivalent, giving us the correct scale of F:

F-G-A-Bb-C-D-E-

CHROMATIC SCALES
WITH DIATONIC SCALES HIGHLIGHTED

1		2		3	4		5		6		7	8
C	C#	D	D#	E	F	F#	G	G#	A	A#	B	C
D	D#	E	F	F#	G	G#	A	A#	B	C	C#	D
Eb	E	F	Gb	G	Ab	A	Bb	B	C	Db	D	Eb
E	F	F#	G	G#	A	A#	B	C	C#	D	D#	E
F	Gb	G	Ab	A	Bb	B	C	Db	D	Eb	E	F
G	G#	A	A#	B	C	C#	D	D#	E	F	F#	G
Ab	A	Bb	B	C	Db	D	Eb	E	F	Gb	G	Ab
A	A#	B	C	C#	D	D#	E	F	F#	G	G#	A
Bb	B	C	Db	D	Eb	E	F	Gb	G	Ab	A	Bb
B	C	C#	D	D#	E	F	F#	G	G#	A	A#	B

Scale steps must have consecutive letters: A-B-C-D-E-F-G.

Rule for diatonic scale steps: 2 whole steps, a half step, 3 whole steps, and a half step. Read scales from left to right. The name of the scale is in column No. 1.

A half step is from one column to the next column. A whole step consists of two half steps.

OTHER KINDS OF SCALES

Although our main interest in chord construction is the diatonic scale, there are many other kinds of scales, sometimes called modes, with names like Dorian, Lydian, Mixolydian, Locrian, Phrygian and our own major scale also known as the Ionian mode. It is interesting that many contemporary musicians frequently employ some of these modes in their solos and songs. Despite such scales sounding peculiar to the ears of Western musicians, they are not unfamiliar in other parts of the world, particularly in India, Eastern Europe and the Middle East. Some Flamenco music, for example, adapts a Phyrigian mode, as does Jewish Klezmer with its Ahava Raba and Freygish scales. The Phrygian scale pattern of 1-2b-3-4-5-6b-7b-1 can readily be heard in songs like *Hava Nagila* and *Misirlou*.

There's also a type of scale called Pentatonic consisting of 5 notes (penta=5, like a five-side pentagon). It's a scale that rock & roll guitar players use to great advantage. The black notes of the keyboard make a perfect Pentatonic scale. Try playing them for the start of Irving Berlin's *Always*, the lovely Chinese song *Shina No Yoro (China Night)*, the Japanese folk song *Sakura*, the Scottish *Auld Lang Syne*, the popular 1925 song *Dinah*, and the opening phrases of *Louise* – "Ev'ry little breeze seems to whisper Louise ..." Try too the folk songs *I Gave My Love A Cherry*, *Oh! Susanna*, and *Five Hundred Miles*.

Yet another scale that is worthy of mention is the WholeTone scale. As the name implies, the distance between steps is a whole tone. There are no semi tones. The result is an octave with six equally distant steps. The sound is haunting, somewhat mysterious. Take a look at the Whole Tone scale of C and its numbers:

$$C-D-E-F\#-G\#-A\#-C$$
$$1-2-3-4\#-5\#-6\#-8$$

Todd Taylor

12

SOME POPULAR CHORDS
AND THEIR SCALE TONES

The chords and their combination of scale tone numbers presented in this section represent some of the most frequently used chords heard today in traditional and contemporary harmony. By no means does this section propose to include every possible chord, but it does include the bulk of them. For these chords and several more popular chords see Table No. 1 (Popular Chord Types, Scale Numbers and C Scale Symbols.) For an expanded list of chords see Table No. 2 (Chord Groups & Diatonic Scale Numbers.)

THE BIG FIVE

MAJOR CHORD: 1-3-5
The major chord is formed by combining the 1st, 3rd, and 5th tones of the diatonic scale. This three tone chord is kown as a triad. It receives its name "major" – just as does the "major" scale -- from the interval between the 1st and 3rd tone, which is technically referred to as "major third." Usually a major chord is called just by its letter name, such as C, F#, or Ab, the word "major, being implied. Its chord symbol uses only the letter name.

MINOR CHORD: 1-3b-5
The minor chord is distinguished from the major chord in that it lowers the 3rd degree of the scale. This flatted 3rd is characteristic of all types of minor chords. Its name stems from the interval between the 1st tone to the flatted 3rd, which is known as a "minor third." Its chord symbol uses the small letter "m" such as Cm for C minor, Bb minor for Bb minor, and Gm for G minor. Sometimes a dash replaces the small "m", for example C-, Bb-, G-. If the 3rd scale tone is a sharp, lower it to the natural tone with the same alphabetical letter name a half step below.

SEVENTH CHORD: 1-3-5-7b
Next to the major and minor chord, the seventh chord is perhaps the most used and the most important. There will often be more seventh chords in a composition than any other chord type. Their sound is very close to a major chord since they are built on the major triad 1-3-5 with the flatted 7th tone added. This chord type is sometimes referred to as a "dominant" seventh. But the symbol for a seventh chord is with a 7 not a 7b. Typical examples are C7, Bb7, and F#7.

DIMINISHED CHORD: 1-3b – 5b
Whereas augment means to increase, diminish means just the opposite, and a diminished chord decreases its 3rd and 5th tones, lowering them by a half-step. It is more common today to use a "diminished seventh" chord than a diminished triad. To see how this chord is constructed first look at a basic seventh chord then lower its 3-5-7b tones. Note that the 7b is flatted again creating what's known as a double flat. (The 7bb is the same as a 6.) Symbols for diminished chords are Cdim (or Cdim7), Bbdim (or Bbdim7). A degree sign is also used like C° and Db°. The minus sign used for minor chords can also indicate a diminished chord.

AUGMENTED FIFTH CHORD: 1-3-5#

To augment means to increase or raise, and that's just what the augmented fifths do: they raise their 5th scalar tone a half-step. The symbol for an augmented chord is usually a "plus" sign such as C+5, G+5, and Bb+5. Variations include Caug5, Gaug5, Bbaug5, or simply the plus sign alone as in C+, G+, and Bb+. As we will see, other types of augmented chords exist, (augmented sevenths and augmented ninths) but their characteristic feature is raising the 5th tone of the scale. If the 5th scale tone is already a sharp, raise it to the next natural scale tone above it. The B+5 chord is spelled B-D#-G. Similarly, if the 5th tone is a flat, raise it to the natural tone with the same alphabetical letter name. The Eb+5 chord is spelled Eb-G-B. (The augmented chord is often used as a steppingstone from the tonic chord to the subdominant chord and from the dominant seventh to the tonic. See:GENERIC CHORDS section for terms.)

THE LITTLE FOUR

SIXTH CHORD: 1-3-5-6

A sixth chord has the sound of a major chord but is fuller and sweeter. It is often used as substitute for the major chord, especially in popular music where it lends a contemporary sound. The chord is formed simply by adding the 6th scalar tone to a major chord. Its symbol is a 6, such as D6, G6, Bb6.

MINOR SEVENTH CHORD: 1-3b-5-7b

This chord is probably one of the most versatile of contemporary popular chords. It can be used as a substitute for many minor triads, especially when they occur in the middle of a progression. Because they have the characteristics of both a minor and a dominant seventh chord, they are frequently substituted for both. Like a regular seventh chord, the flatted 7th tone gives the chord a transitional feeling, that is, it helps the chord to move smoothly to the next chord. The chord creates a sweeter sound than the somewhat harsher sounding minor triad. Typical symbols are Dm7, Ebm7, and Cm7.

MAJOR SEVENTH CHORD: 1-3-5-7

Despite its name, this chord is not a substitute for the regular seventh chord. The strident addition of a natural 7th tone – not a flatted 7th – to a major triad produces a powerful substitute for the major triad. Distinctly "modern" in its sound, it was rarely heard in popular music until its appearance in recent years. It can support a melody note that effectively starts on the unflatted 7th tone as in It Had To Be You and When It's Sleepy Time Down South. It can also figure prominently in songs like Laura, Misty, and Duke Ellington's Solitude. Standard symbols are CM7, GM7, Fmaj7, and Dmaj7 and occasionally a triangle such as CΔ.

NINTH CHORD: 1-3-5-7b-9

Essentially a seventh chord with the 9th scale tone added, the ninth chord can often be used as a substitute for the seventh chord giving it a fuller, richer sound. Check out the jazz standard There'll Be Some Changes Made. It opens with several ninth chords.

LET'S MAKE A CHORD

Just follow these basic steps:

1) Determine the chord you want to make.

2) From Table No. 1 (Popular Chord Types, Scale Numbers and C Scale Symbols) determine the necessary scale numbers.

3) From the chart of DIATONIC SCALES AND TONE NUMBERS, select the scale that has the same letter name as the desired chord, such as C or G or Bb or F, etc.

4) From the chart of DIATONIC SCALES AND TONE NUMBERS, select the required scale tones.

5) Using the keyboard or fretboard diagrams, apply the appropriate scale tones using coins or other objects.

Let's make a C7 chord:

1) From Table No. 1 (Popular Chord Types) we see that we need the 1-3-5-7b tones for a seventh chord.

2) The letter name of the chord is C, so we refer to the C scale in the chart of Diatonic Scales.

3) From the C scale select the 1-3-5-7 tones, flat the 7, and we have C-E-G-Bb.

4) Apply those letter tones to the appropriate fingerboard or keyboard diagram in a playable arrangement.

Let's make a G chord:

1) From Table No. 1 (Popular Chord Types) we see that we need the 1-3-5 tones for a major chord.

2) The letter name of the chord is G so we refer to the G scale in the chart of Diatonic Scales .

3) From the G scale select the 1-3-5 tones which are G-B-D.

4) Apply those letter tones to the appropriate diagram.

Let's make a Bbm7 chord:

1) From Table No. 1 (Popular Chord Types) we see that we need the 1-3b-5-7b tones for a minor seventh chord.

2) The letter name of the chord is Bb so we refer to the Bb scale in the chart of Diatonic scales.

3) From the Bb scale select the 1-3-5-7 tones, flat the 3 and the 7th, which gives us Bb-Db-F-Ab.

4) Apply those letters to the appropriate diagram.

Let's make an Fdim7 chord:

1) From Table No. 1 (Popular Chord Types) we see that we need the 1-3b-5b-7bb for a diminished seventh chord.

2) The letter name of the chord is F so we refer to the F scale in the chart of Diatonic Scales.

3) From the F scale we select the 1-3-5-7 tones, flat the 3 and 5, and double flat the 7, which gives us F-Ab-B-D.

4) Apply those letter tones to the appropriate diagram.

Let's make a D9 chord:

1) From Table No. 1 (Popular Chord Types) we see that we need the 1-3-5-7b-9 for a ninth chord.

2) The letter name of the chord is D so we refer to the D scale in the chart of Diatonic Scales.

3) From the F scale we select the 1-3-5-7-9 tones, flat the 7th, which give us D-F#-A-C-E.

4) Apply those letter tones to the appropriate diagram.

Let's make a C7+5 chord:

1) From Table No. 1 (Popular Chord Types) we see that we need the 1-3-5#-7b for an augmented seventh chord.

2) the letter name of the chord is C so we refer to the C scale in the chart of Diatonic Scales.

3) From the C scale we select the 1-3-5-7 tones, sharp the 5th and flat the seventh, which gives us C-E-G#-Bb.

4) Apply those letter tones to the appropriate diagram.

Johnny Smith

TABLE NO. 1

Popular Chord Types
Scale Numbers and C Chord Symbols

CHORD TYPE	SCALE NUMBERS	SYMBOLS
Major triad	*(1-3-5)*	*C*
Major sixth	*1-3-5-6*	*C6*
Major seventh	*1-3-5-7*	*CM7, Cmaj7*
Major ninth	*1-3-5-9*	*CM9, Cmaj9*
Minor triad	*1-3b-5*	*Cm, C-*
Minor sixth	*1-3b-5-6*	*Cm6, C-6*
Minor seventh	*1-3b-5-7b*	*Cm7, C-7*
Minor/Major seventh	*1-3b-5-7*	*Cm/maj7*
Seventh	*1-3-5-7b*	*C7*
Ninth	*1-3-5-7b-9*	*C9*
Diminished triad	*1-3b-5b*	*Cdim, C⁻*
Diminished seventh	*1-3b-5b-7bb*	*Cdim7, C⁻ 7*
Augmented triad	*1-3-5#*	*C+, C+5, Caug, Caug5*
Augmented seventh	*1-3-5#-7b*	*C7aug, C7aug5, C7+5*
Augmented ninth	*1-3-5#-7b-9*	*C9aug, C9 aug5, C9+5*

SOME GENERAL RULES:
Minor chords flat the 3rd.
Seventh and ninth chords flat the 7th.
Augmented chords raise the 5th.
Diminished triads lower the 3rd and 5th.
Diminished seventh chords lower the 3rd, 5th, and flatted 7th.
Chords with a number in their name should always include that numbered tone.

DIATONIC SCALES AND TONE NUMBERS

	1	2	3	4	5	6	7	8 octave	9
C scale	C	D	E	F	G	A	B	C	D
C# scale	C#	D#	E#	F#	G#	A#	B#	C#	D#
Db scale	Db	Eb	F	Gb	Ab	Bb	C	Db	E
D scale	D	E	F#	G	A	B	C#	D	E
Eb scale	Eb	F	G	Ab	Bb	C	D	Eb	F
E scale	E	F#	G#	A	B	C#	D#	E	F#
F scale	F	G	A	Bb	C	D	E	F	G
F# scale	F#	G#	A#	B	C#	D#	E#	F#	G#
G scale	G	A	B	C	D	E	F#	G	A
Ab scale	Ab	Bb	C	Db	Eb	F	G	Ab	Bb
A scale	A	B	C#	D	E	F#	G#	A	B
Bb scale	Bb	C	D	Eb	F	G	A	Bb	C
B scale	B	C#	D#	E	F#	G#	A#	B	C#

The scales shown here are those most frequently used in chord construction.
Note: In the C# and F#scales an E# is used instead of an F to preserve the consecutive alphabetical order. So too in the C# scale a B# is used instead of a C.
For chords using tone numbers higher than 9, the octave of 3=10, the octave of 4=11, the octave of 5=12, the octave of 6=13.
The C# and Db scales are enharmonic, meaning they have the same pitch but different names.

TABLE NO. 2
CHORD GROUPS & DIATONIC SCALE NUMBERS

MAJOR:

Major triad	1-3-5
Major sixth	1-3-5-6
Major seventh	1-3-5-7
Major ninth	1-3-5-9
Major sixth/major ninth	1-3-5-6-9 (a "six-nine" chord
Major seventh/major ninth	1-3-5-7-9
Major ninth/augmented eleventh	1-3-5-9-11#

MINOR:

Minor triad	1-3b-5
Minor sixth	1-3b-5-6
Minor/major seventh	1-3b-5-7
Minor sixth/major ninth	1-3b-5-6-9
Minor/major seventh/ major ninth	1-3b-5-7-9

SEVENTH: (Sometimes referred to as a "Dominant" Seventh.

Seventh	1-3-5-7b
Ninth	1-3-5-7b-9
Eleventh	1-3-5-7b-9-11
Thirteenth	1-3-5-7b-9-11-13
"Seven/Six)" (abbreviated thirteenth)	1-3-5-7b-13

MINOR SEVENTH:

Minor seventh	1-3b-5-7b
Minor ninth	1-3b-5-7b-9
Minor eleventh	1-3b-5-7b-9-11
Minor thirteenth	1-3b-5-7b-9-11-13

AUGMENTED:

Augmented triad	1-3-5#
Seventh augmented fifth	1-3-5# -7b
Ninth augmented fifth	1-3-5# -7b-9
Major ninth augmented fifth	1-3-5# -9

DIMINISHED:

Diminished triad	1-3b-5b
Diminished seventh	1-3b-5b-7bb
Half-diminished seventh	1-3b-5b-7b

Note: The chart of DIATONIC SCALES AND TONE NUMBERS only goes up to the 9th tone.
For chords with numbers above 9 continue the scale steps consecutively for 10, 11, and 13.
Fretboard diagrams go up the 5th fret. For higher frets use the blank diagram and enter the tones
consecutively on each string.

MODERN JAZZ CHORDING

Less common chords can be found in contemporary jazz scores, but whatever the chord name the rules for forming it by scale numbers remains the same. Diatonic chord charts in this book go up to the 9th scalar tone. For anything beyond that -- say tones based on steps 10, 11, or 13 -- just continue in stepwise fashion from 9. Whereas 9 is an octave above the 2nd step of the scale, the 10th tone is an octave above the 3rd step, the 11th the 4th step, and the 13th the 6th. For general reference, here's a sample of some modern chords with their C scale symbols, numbers, and tones. Be prepared: some are quite dissonant. As you can imagine, there are an infinite variety of unusual "weird" chords. Optional tones are in parentheses.

Minor six/nine	Cm6/9	1-3b-(5)-6-9	C-Eb-(G)-A -D
Minor seventh flat 5	Cm7b5	1-3b-5b-7b	C-Eb-Gb-Bb
Seventh flat 5	C7b5	1-3-5b-7b	C-E-Gb-Bb
Seventh flat 9	C7b9	1-3-5-7b-9b	C-E-G-Bb-Db
Seventh sharp 9	C7#9	1-3-5-7b-9#	C-E-G-Bb-D#
Seventh flat 13	C7b13	1-3-5-7b-13b	C-E-G-Bb-Ab
Seventh suspended 4	C7sus4	1-4-5-7b	C-F-G-Bb
Eleventh	C11	1-(3-5)-7b-9-11	C-(E-G)-Bb-D-F
Thirteenth	C13	1-(3-5)-7b-9-11-13	C-(E-G)-Bb-D-F-A

ELIMINATING CHORD TONES

If a chord has more tones than the number of strings on an instrument, or if inserting all the required tones isn't feasible, some tones can be eliminated while still preserving the essential sound of the chord. Here are a few tips: Try to keep the root tone, that is, the tone that has the same alphabetical letter name as the chord. If the chord calls for a 7b, make sure it is included. Minor chords must have a 3b, otherwise the 3 tone can often be eliminated. The 5th scalar tone is sometimes weak and can also be dropped. If the chord has a number in its name like a sixth chord, or a ninth, or an augmented fifth, be sure those nunmber tones are included. In the final analysis, *let your ear be your guide.*

INVERSIONS

The re-arrangement of chord tones is called an inversion. A seventh chord with the tones 1-3-5-7b would still be the same chord if we turned those tones around in a different order like 5-3-1-7b or 1-5-3-7b or any other juxtaposition. The sound of these inverted chords is slightly different even though they contain the same tones. Low tones become high tones and vice versa. Sometimes deciding the name of a chord you are listening to can be elusive only to find it's an inversion of a basic chord.

Try experimenting with different inversions to hear their sound for yourself. You'll find that sometimes the harmony of an inverted chord can add just the right touch.

In formal music inversions have specific names, but for our purposes it suffices just to know that chord tones can be flip-flopped, turned upside down, and still preserve their essential sound but with a new twist emphasizing a particular tone of the chord.

GENERIC CHORDS

In addition to identifying chords by their conventional names, chords can have an alternate WORD and ROMAN NUMERAL name. Here's a list of such names, the scale steps on which they are based, and their chord letter names in the scale (key) of C.

WORD NAME	ROMAN NUMERAL*	SCALE STEP	LETTER NAME
Tonic	I	First	C
Supertonic	II	Second	D
Mediant	III	Third	E
Subdominant	IV	Fourth	F
Dominant	V	Fifth	G
Superdominant	VI	Sixth	A
Leading	VII	Seventh	B

*Major chords are indicated with large Roman numerals.
Minor chords are indicated with small Roman numerals: i-ii-iii-iv-v-vi-vii.

Chord TYPES (seventh, sixth, ninth, etc.) are added to the Roman numerals.
In the key (scale) of C a I7 chord is a C7, a ii7 is a Dm7, a V9 is a G9, etc.

 The advantage of using numbers to identify chords is that they are GENERIC and can be applied to any key without specifying the actual chords by name. A chord progression of I-IV-V can be a C-F-G in the key of C, or a G-C-D in the key of G, or an A-D-E in the key of A.

 Bluegrass and folk players somtimes use fingers to indicate basic 1-4-5
(I-IV-V) accompaniment chords for beginners -- one finger, four fingers, five fingers.

HOW TO USE GENERIC CHORDS

12-Bar Blues in the Key of Bb

4/4 Bb	F7	Bb	Bb7
Eb	Ebm	Bb/D7	G7
C7	F7	Bb/Eb7	Bb

Same Song in Generic Format

4/4 I	V7	I	I7
IV	iv	I/III7	VI7
II7	V7	I/IV7	I

To play this song in any key, apply the Roman numerals to the scale of the key you want to play in. In the key of F, for example, select the F diatonic scale. Notice how in the 6th measure (bar) the small Roman numeral is used for the minor chord. If Roman numerals are too confusing, try using Arabic numbers. Here are the chords following the generic format:

Same Song in the Key of F

4/4 F	C7	F	F7
Bb	Bbm	F/A7	D7
G7	C7	F/Bb7	F

Same Song in the Key of C

4/4 C	G7	C	C7
F	Fm	C/E7	A7
D7	G7	C/F7	C

Let's take another example with a more expanded chord progression:

Let Me Call You Sweetheart (Key of C)

3/4 C	C	C	C
F	A7	D7	D7
G7	G7	G7	G7
C	C#dim7	G7	G7
C	C	C	C
F	A7	Dm	Dm
F	F#dim7	C	A7
D7	G7	C	C

Same Song in Generic Format (Any Key)

3/4 I	I	I	I
IV	VI7	II7	II7
V7	V7	V7	V7
I	I#dim7	V7	V7
I	I	I	I
IV	VI7	ii	ii
IV	IV#dim7	I	VI7
II7	V7	I	I

Challenge: Can you transpose this song to another key? How about the key of G or the key of F? Clue: Use the chart of Diatonic Scales and Tone Numbers. Choose a scale that has the same letter name as the key you want, then determine the letter names of the chords that correspond to the generic Roman numerals.

GUIDELINES
FOR SUCCESSFUL FRETBOARD BINGO

1) Don't put more than one tone on the same string.

2) Don't play the sa me note on adjacent strings.

3) Take full advantage of open strings that don't have to be fingered. Avoid using high notes and low open-string notes in the same chord.

4) Listen to the voicing of the chord. Does it sound pleasant?

5) On fretted instruments, keep chord tones close together. Don't spread tones more than 3 or 4 frets. On keyboard instruments there's more latitude and chords can be played "open" with tones spread apart or "closed" with tones tight together.

6) Use coins – heads & tails – to indicate certain tones. For example, use heads to indicate roots (See Useful Chord Terms for "Root"). Try also using different varieties of coins for certain tones, such as pennies for roots, nickels for 3rds, dimes for 5ths, etc.

7) Look for movable chords. Chords that do not have an open string can be moved up or down. But all tones must be moved in the same direction and for the same distance. The chord's letter name will change to that of the new root.

8) Use all strings on 4-string instruments. Don't skip strings. On the 5-string banjo don't play the 5th string unless it's a drone or one of the chord tones.

9) On the guitar, start by playing the top four strings. Then add the 5th and 6th string if you can finger them.

10) Make sure the chord is playable. If necessary re-arrange tones for easier fingering.

NOTE: To make a chord playable, sometimes it's necessary to eliminate one or more of the prescribed chord tones. Try not to remove the root tone or the 3rd. If it's a minor chord be sure to keep the flatted 3rd. If there's a number in the chord name – like 6,7, or 9 – be sure to keep that tone. Chord tones can be doubled but keep them an octave apart.

USEFUL CHORD TERMS

ADDED CHORD: A basic chord type, such as a triad or seventh, to which certain other tones have been added. The ninth chord is an added chord. It adds the 9th tone to the seventh chord.

ALTERED CHORD: A variation of a chord that raises or lowers one or more of its tones. The augmented fifth chord raises the 5th tone. A diminished seventh chord lowers all its tones except the root.

CHORD PROGRESSION: A series of chords. The ii7-V7-I progression in the key of C is Dm7-G7-C.

CHROMATIC SCALE: A 12-note scale consisting entirely of consecutive half-steps.

DIATONIC SCALE: An 8-note scale consisting of whole steps and half steps in the sequence of 2-½-3-½.

DOMINANT SEVENTH: The seventh chord that flats the 7th tone, as in 1-3-5-7b.

ENHARMONIC: A term applied to different names for the same pitch. Eb and D# are enharmonic tones. So too are C# and Db. Black notes on the keyboard have enhamonic names, either a sharp or a flat.

EXTENDED CHORD: A chord that adds 9th, 11th, or 13th scale tones beyond the 7th.

FIVE CHORD: Chords are sometimes identified by the NUMBER of the scale tone on which they are built. A "five" chord would be built on the 5th tone of a scale, a "six" chord on the 6th scale tone. Roman numerals are used to indicate the chord number.

FLATTING A TONE: If the tone is a sharp, when it's flatted it goes to a natural tone. Thus a C# becomes a C natural, an F# becomes an F. If the tone is a flat, like a Bb, when it's flatted it becomes a "double flat" and drops to the next lower tone on the scale. Thus a Bbb becomes an A.

INVERSION: A different way to arrange the order of tones for the same chord. C-E-G, G-C-E, and E-C-G are all inversion of the same C chord.

KEY: The tonality of a musical composition, based on the scale step that shares its name. The key of C is based on a C scale. Each scale step has a corresponding key.

MAJOR SEVENTH: a seventh chord that does not flat the 7th tone, as in 1-3-5-7. The 7th tone is a natural.

NATURAL TONE: A tone that is neither sharped nor flatted.

OCTAVE: A musical interval spanning eight tones.

ROOT: A chord's root is the fundamental tone on which the chord is constructed. It is the root tone that gives a chord its letter name. The root of a C chord is the C tone.

SCALE: A ladder-like series of tones arranged in either ascending or descending order according to prescribed intervals of whole steps and half steps.

SLASH CHORD: A chord followed by a slash mark and a letter name, like Dm7/F. The letter following the slash indicates the lowest tone of the chord. This bass tone can be one of the chord tones or a tone not part of the chord, like a Dm7/B which is a Dm7 chord with a B in the bass position.

TRIAD: A 3-tone chord.

ALTERNATE TUNINGS

Individual diagrams are provided for both keyboard and the most popular fretted instruments. In addition a blank form is included so you can make your own diagram for other instruments or alternate tunings. In the following examples, read tuning notes from left to right, low to high:

4-String Banjo, Guitar tuning: DGBE

    (Same as baritone ukulele)

4-String Banjo, Irish tuning: GDAE

    (Same as mandolin)

4-String Mountain Dulcimer: CGCC

5-String Banjo, C tuning: gCGBD

    (Sometimes referred to as Classic Banjo tuning)

5-String Banjo, G modal tuning: gDGCD

5-String Banjo, Double C tuning: gCGCD

5-String Banjo, D tuning: f#DF#AD

6-String Banjo: EADGBE

    (Same as guitar)

Guitar, D tuning: DADF#AD

Guitar, Slack Key G tuning: DGDGD

Dobro, G tuning: GBDGBD

12-String Guitar: eE-aA-dD-gG-BB-EE

    (Low strings are tuned in octaves, high strings in unison)

Mandola: CGDA

    (Same as tenor banjo or Irish GDAE)

Tenor Guitar: CGDA

    (Same as tenor banjo)

Balalaika: EEA

Lutes - Medieval, Renaissance, and Baroque: frets are tied nylon or gut strings.
    (6, 7, or 8 courses in various tunings)

5-STRING BANJO
G TUNING

5TH STRING	4TH STRING	3RD STRING	2ND STRING	1ST STRING	
G	D	G	B	D	OPEN STRING
G#/Ab	D#/Eb	G#/Ab	C	D#/Eb	1ST FRET
A	E	A	C#/Db	E	2ND FRET
A#/Bb	F	A#/Bb	D	F	3RD FRET
B	F#/Gb	B	D#/Eb	F#/Gb	4TH FRET
C	G	C	E	G	5TH FRET

PELCTRUM BANJO

4TH STRING	3RD STRING	2ND STRING	1ST STRING	
C	G	B	D	OPEN STRING
C#/Db	G#/Ab	C	D#/Eb	1ST FRET
D	A	C#/Db	E	2ND FRET
D#/Eb	A#/Bb	D	F	3RD FRET
E	B	D#/Eb	F#/Gb	4TH FRET
F	C	E	G	5TH FRET

TENOR BANJO

4TH STRING	3RD STRING	2ND STRING	1ST STRING	
C	G	D	A	OPEN STRING
C#/Db	G#/Ab	D#/Eb	A#/Bb	1ST FRET
D	A	E	B	2ND FRET
D#/Eb	A#/Bb	F	C	3RD FRET
E	B	F#/Gb	C#/Db	4TH FRET
F	C	G	D	5TH FRET

GUITAR

6TH STRING	5TH STRING	4TH STRING	3RD STRING	2ND STRING	1ST STRING	
E	A	D	G	B	E	OPEN STRING
F	A#/Bb	D#/Eb	G#/Ab	C	F	1ST FRET
F#/Gb	B	E	A	C#/Db	F#/Gb	2ND FRET
G	C	F	A#/Bb	D	G	3RD FRET
G#/Ab	C#/Db	F#/Gb	B	D#/Eb	G#/Ab	4TH FRET
A	D	G	C	E	A	5TH FRET

MANDOLIN

4TH STRING	3RD STRING	2ND STRING	1ST STRING	
G	D	A	E	OPEN STRING
G#/A^b	D#/E^b	A#/B^b	F	1ST FRET
A	E	B	F#/G^b	2ND FRET
A#/B^b	F	C	G	3RD FRET
B	F#/G^b	C#/D^b	G#/A^b	4TH FRET
C	G	D	A	5TH FRET

BARITONE UKULELE

4TH STRING	3RD STRING	2ND STRING	1ST STRING	
D	G	B	E	OPEN STRING
D#/E♭	G#/A♭	C	F	1ST FRET
E	A	C#/D♭	F#/G♭	2ND FRET
F	A#/B♭	D	G	3RD FRET
F#/G♭	B	D#/E♭	G#/A♭	4TH FRET
G	C	E	A	5TH FRET

SOPRANO, CONCERT & TENOR UKULELES

4TH STRING	3RD STRING	2ND STRING	1ST STRING	
G	C	E	A	OPEN STRING
G#/A♭	C#/D♭	F	A#/B♭	1ST FRET
A	D	F#/G♭	B	2ND FRET
A#/B♭	D#/E♭	G	C	3RD FRET
B	E	G#/A♭	C#/D♭	4TH FRET
C	F	A	D	5TH FRET

BLANK CHART

6TH STRING	5TH STRING	4TH STRING	3RD STRING	2ND STRING	1ST STRING	
◯	◯	◯	◯	◯	◯	OPEN STRING
						1ST FRET
						2ND FRET
						3RD FRET
						4TH FRET
						5TH FRET

KEYBOARD DIAGRAM

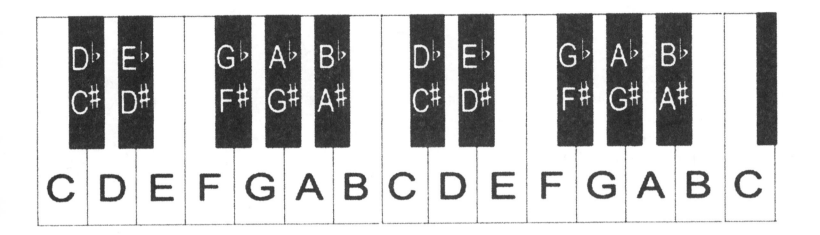

THE AUTHOR REFLECTS

Dick Sheridan's attractions to chords began as a pre-teenager when a small soprano ukulele was given to him for a Christmas present. The song book that came with the ukulele had melodies written in standard notation with a fingerboard diagram placed above every note. Dots were put on the strings to indicate where the fingers should be placed to sound each note. It was a cumbersome, tedious system and Dick rapidly lost interest. Up on a closet shelf went the ukulele along with the song book, extra strings, and a large soft green felt ukulele pick.

The following summer, probably in the throes of youthful boredom, down from the closet shelf came the ukulele and song book. But this time Dick noticed something different: below the melody line and its note-for-note diagrams, there were other diagrams widely spaced apart some of which contained two or more finger dots. Rather than playing one string at a time, the directions were to play all strings simultaneously.

A chord!

Dick was intrigued by the sound, the harmony, an exciting world of music had opened up, and the fascination with chords has never ceased.

During high school years Dick accompanied himself with chords on an acoustic folk guitar, then it was on to college with a baritone uke for pep rallies and dorm sessions. Concurrently he was recruited to play tenor banjo with a campus Dixieland jazz band. He continues to play banjo with a traditional jazz band, a six piece group he leads and has played with for over 50 years.

The underlying common denominator of all these activities, past and present, has been the enjoyment of chords. It is this interest – obsession might be a better word – that brings us to CHORD BINGO.

Let Dick tell the story in his own words:

> *Chord Bingo has been long in the making. The project was started in the late 1960s, and when I had the opportunity to travel to Europe in 1970 I took it with me to a British magazine called B.M.G. (for Banjo, Mandolin, and Guitar). I was hopeful they'd be interested in publishing it, but unfortunately the firm was in a state of some disarray owing to the recent passing of a principal member. Despite much encouragement to press on, I set my notes aside only occasionally bringing them out, refining them, and adding new material. But essentially the project languished.*

Then, some 30 years later at a gathering of the American Banjo Fraternity in upstate New York, I met again by chance my contact from B.M.G. who was visitng from London. When we rekindled our acquaintance, the first thing he said was "Whatever did you do with that game called Chord Bingo?" Surprisingly after all those intervening years he had remembered it, and that proved the impetus needed to reconsider the project, dust it off, and bring it up to date.

When Chord Bingo was first drafted all of the text was done on newsprint with a typewriter, the charts and diagrams all hand drawn and lettered. Times have changed, and now thanks to the computer and its graphic capabilities, everything has been reorganzied, revitalized, and made more presentable. Assembling new material along with the accumulation of revisions, marginal notes, and inserts has proved something of an ongoing challenge, but the results I feel have been well worth the effort.

Fortunately chord theory has remained essentially unchanged. The rules of how chords are constructed have not been altered, although the infusion of modern chording may cause some traditionalists to throw up their hands in dispair.

When Chord Bingo was initially created I was not doing much by way of private music teaching. In subsequent years that has significantly changed. Working with students on various chord instruments has since brought the opportunity of putting Chord Bingo to use. The results have indeed been gratifying. Chord theory has come alive for students, as well as for musical colleagues whose understanding of chords has been limited, confusing, and something of a mystery.

I'm sure you'll find the contents of this book not only interesting but useful, fun, and rewarding. New sounds are waiting to be heard, new chord positions to be made and played. Whatever your instrument, your understanding of chords will serve you well and bring the lifelong satisfaction that comes with knowledge and its application.

More Great Books from Dick Sheridan...

**CELTIC SONGS
FOR THE TENOR BANJO** `INCLUDES TAB`
37 Traditional Songs and Instrumentals
by Dick Sheridan

Jigs & reels, hornpipes, airs, dances and more are showcased in this exciting 37 collection drawn from Ireland, Scotland, Wales, Cornwall, Brittany and the Isle of Man. Each traditional song – with its lilting melody and rich accompaniment harmony – has been carefully selected and presented for tenor banjo in both note form and tablature with chord symbols and diagrams. Lyrics and extra verses are included for many songs. Includes: All Through The Night, Blackbird Will You Go, The Campbells Are Coming, Garry Owen, Harvest Home, O'Gallaher's Frolics, Saddle The Pony, Swallow Tail Jig and many more.
00122477..$14.99

**LOVE SONGS
FOR UKULELE** `INCLUDES TAB`
37 Love Songs in All
by Dick Sheridan

Romance is in the air, and here to prove it are 37 of the best and most enduring love songs ever! Here are romantic treasures from the musical theater; whimsical novelty numbers; ballads of both true and false love; songs for sweethearts, lovers and hopefuls; sad songs of longing and heartbreak; and barbershop favorites. The creative ukulele arrangements in notes, tab & chords make each song rewarding and fun to play. Includes: Beautiful Dreamer • Careless Love • I Love You Truly • Let Me Call You Sweetheart • My Gal Sal • Avalon • Frankie and Johnny • Secrets • Margie • Oh By Jingo! • I Want a Girl • Ida • Moonlight Bay • and many more. Arranged in standard C tuning for soprano, concert and tenor ukuleles, with tunes readily adaptable to baritone ukulele, tenor guitars, and guitar-tuned banjos.
00119342..$12.99

HALLELUJAH UKULELE `INCLUDES TAB`
19 of the Best and Most Beloved Hymns & Spirituals
by Dick Sheridan

Here's a truly special collection of gospel favorites drawn from the traditions of many faiths and cultures. It brings a delightful mix of treasured worship songs, including: Amazing Grace • Go Down, Moses • Hine Mah Tev • In the Garden • The Old Rugged Cross • Rock My Soul • Swing Low, Sweet Chariot • What a Friend We Have in Jesus • and many more. This book contains basic melodies with notes and tablature, exciting creative harmonies, chord symbols and large, easy-to-read diagrams, and selected solos and lyrics.
00122113..$12.99

**YULETIDE FAVORITES
FOR UKULELE** `INCLUDES TAB`
A Treasury of Christmas Hymns, Carols & Songs
by Dick Sheridan

This holiday collection for uke features easy-to-read arrangements with melody in standard notation, tablature, lyrics, chord symbols and diagrams. Selections include traditional American and English carols as well as songs from other countries. Seasonal and holiday tunes are featured, as well as wassails, ancient airs and dances.
00109749..$9.99

**IRISH SONGS
FOR UKULELE** `INCLUDES TAB`
by Dick Sheridan

Shamrocks, shillelaghs and shenanigans...they are all here in this collection of 55 fabulous Irish favorites! Each song is specifically arranged for the ukulele, with the melody in both standard notation and easy-to-read tab. Includes: An Irish Lullaby • The Band Played On • Cockles and Mussels • Danny Boy • The Irish Rover • McNamara's Band • Peg O' My Heart • The Rose of Tralee • and dozens more.
00103153...$15.99

**COLLEGE FIGHT SONGS
& ALMA MATERS FOR UKULELE** `INCLUDES TAB`
by Dick Sheridan

For the varsity football enthusiast, as well as for the perennial college sophomore, here are over 40 of the best-known team songs from major confernences all across the country in easy-to-play arrangements for the ever-popular ukulele. Even if your own school connection is not included, you'll recognize many of these songs made popular through sporting events, radio and TV broadcasts. Includes arrangements in standard notation and tablature, with lyrics and melodies.
00124458...$15.99

**SONGS OF THE CIVIL WAR
FOR UKULELE** `INCLUDES TAB`
by Dick Sheridan

25 tunes of the era that boosted morale, championed causes, pulled on the heartstrings, or gave impetus to battle. Includes: All Quiet Along the Potomac, Aura Lee, Battle Hymn of the Republic, Dixie, The Girl I Left Behind Me, John Brown's Body, When Johnny Comes Marching Home and more - all in standard C tuning, with notation, tablature and accompanying lyrics. The book also includes notes on the songs, historical commentary, and a handy chord chart!
00001588...$14.99

CENTERSTREAM®

P.O. Box 17878 - Anaheim Hills, CA 92817
(714) 779-9390   www.centerstream-usa.com

The Original and Still the Best...

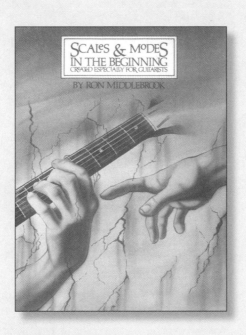

SCALES & MODES IN THE BEGINNING
by Ron Middlebrook
The most comprehensive and complete scale book written especially for the guitar. Chapers include: Fretboard Visualization, Scale Terminology, Scales and Modes, and a Scale to Chord Guide.
00000010..$11.99

P.O. Box 17878 - Anaheim Hills, CA 92817
(714) 779-9390 | www.centerstream-usa.com | centerstrm@aol.com